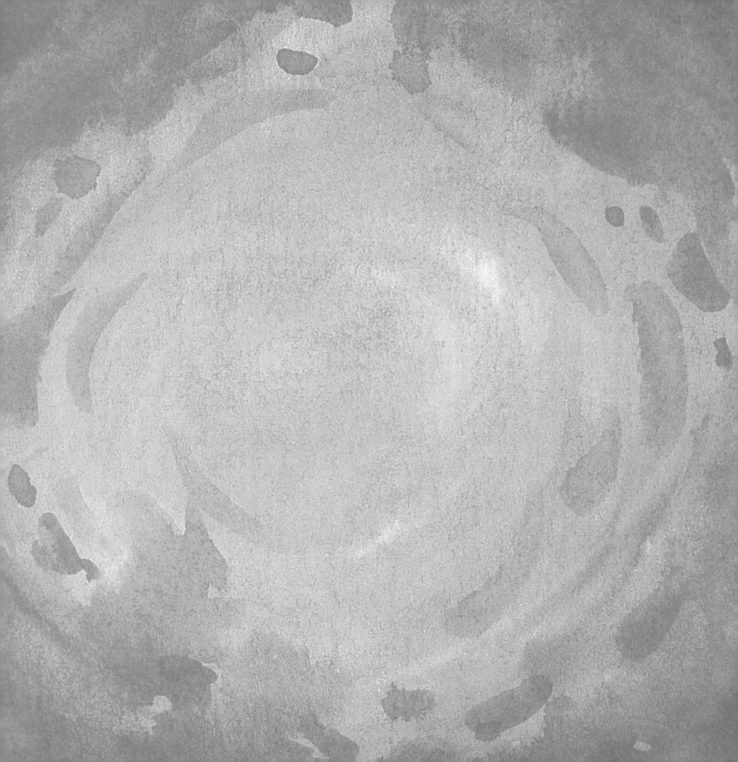

I AM PEACE

A BOOK of MINDFULNESS

BY SUSAN VERDE · ART BY PETER H. REYNOLDS

Abrams Books for Young Readers · New York

For my father, J.L.R.
You will always be
in the here and now.
—S.V.

For my sisters,
Jane and Renee.
—P.H.R.

The illustrations in this book were created using ink, gouache, watercolor, and tea.

Cataloging-in-Publication Data has been applied for
and may be obtained from the Library of Congress.
ISBN 978-1-4197-2701-6

Printed and bound in U.S.A.
10 9 8 7 6 5

Abrams Books for Young Readers are available at special discounts when purchased in
quantity for premiums and promotions as well as fundraising or educational use.
Special editions can also be created to specification. For details, contact
specialsales@abramsbooks.com or the address below.

ABRAMS The Art of Books
195 Broadway, New York, NY 10007
abramsbooks.com

There are times
when I worry about
what might happen next
and what happened before.

The thoughts in my head
are like rushing water

and I feel like a boat

with no anchor...

...being carried away.

I give myself a moment. I take a breath.

And then I tell myself: It's alright.

I feel the ground beneath my feet and steady myself

and start to notice

the HERE

and the NOW.

My thoughts begin to settle. My mind begins to clear.

I am Peace.

I can watch my worries gently pop and disappear.
I let things go.

I can say what I feel *inside* out loud.

I know myself.

I can share kindness
with others.

I make
a difference.

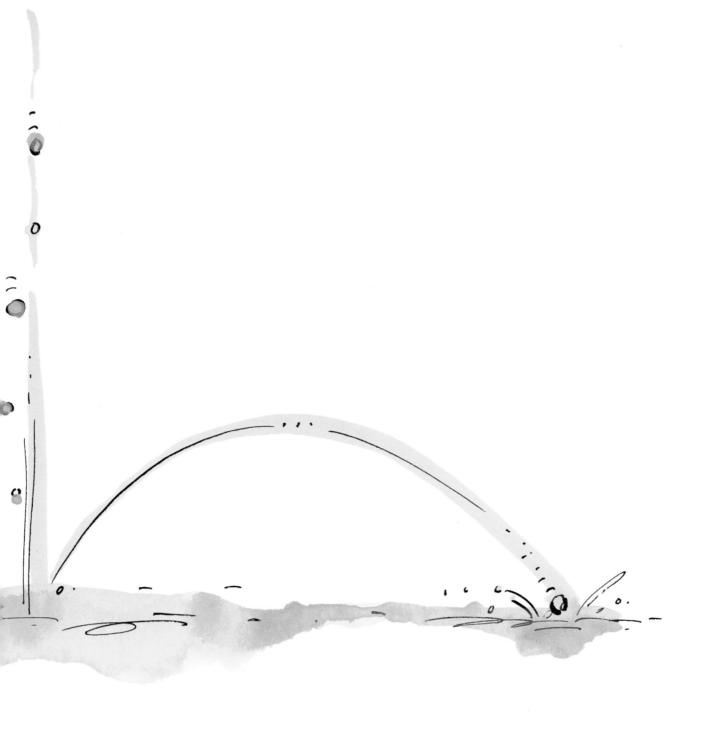

I can hug a tree
and thank it for its beauty
and strength.

I connect to nature.

I can watch the clouds make
shapes against the sky.

I know wonder.

I can taste and smell and touch and hear and see what is all around me. I use my senses.

I can feel my breath
fill my whole body.
I tune into me.

Now the water is still.
I have found my anchor,
and everything IS alright.

I don't need to worry about
before or after.
I am in THIS moment.
I am peace.

Now I share my peace
with others

and hope that it is
carried away
to those who need it.

And I dream...

WE ARE PEACE.

Author's Note

Children have a lot to navigate in this world. They are learning how to make good choices and manage their emotions. They are learning how to be kind to themselves and others while keeping up with schoolwork and balancing their busy lives. Practicing what is known as *mindfulness* can give kids (of all ages) the tools to help them on their journey.

We all have moments of mindfulness in our everyday lives. For example, when we notice the sensation of sand between our toes or the butterflies in our stomachs when we are nervous or excited. When we give someone our undivided attention in conversation, or when we slowly savor our food, we are being mindful. But what does this word actually mean, and why is it important?

Mindfulness means being fully engaged in the present moment, paying careful attention to our experience (our feelings, sensations in the body, emotions, surroundings) without judgment, but with kindness and curiosity. Research shows there are many benefits to practicing mindfulness. There is a great deal of scientific evidence supporting the positive effects on the brain and the body. Being mindful can help one to access parts of the mind that deal with focus, decision-making, and self-regulation. Teaching mindfulness exercises not only strengthens a child's "attention muscle," but it also helps him or her to learn to create distance between their big emotions and themselves. Children develop the ability to *choose* their responses rather than react.

When we learn to be in the here and now, we understand ourselves better, we see beauty, and we act with kindness, compassion, and empathy. When we learn to pause and be present, we find our calm, our center, and our peace. When we feel our own sense of peace, we can share it with others. *I Am Peace* is a reflection of the power of mindfulness in all of our lives.

Guided Meditation

Mindfulness exercises are simple and fun. Here is a mindful meditation that adults and kids can practice together to find their peace.

One of the easiest and most common mindfulness exercises is learning how to focus on our breath. We are always breathing, but we don't always pay attention to how we do it. Noticing our breath helps us connect with sensations in our bodies. By learning how to regulate our breath, we can feel calmer and more grounded in the present moment—this can ultimately help us handle what life sends our way on a daily basis.

Begin by either lying down or finding a comfortable seat. Close your eyes and gently place your hands on your belly. Notice your breathing at this very moment. Is it fast or slow? Can you feel it filling your belly as you breathe in?

Lift a hand and place it in front of your mouth. When you breathe out, what does the air feel like on your hand? Is it warm? Cool? Just notice. There is no right or wrong answer.

With both hands back on your belly, start breathing in through your nose if you weren't already. This will help slow down your breathing and filter the air going into your body.

Imagine your belly is like the ocean. With each inhale, the waves rise, and with each exhale, they fall. Feel your belly rising and falling as you breathe.

Now imagine there is a small boat on your ocean (belly). What does it look like? You don't want the boat to capsize, but you do want to help guide it toward the shore. You can do this by taking nice, slow, deep breaths in and out through your nose. Create a steady rhythm for your boat by breathing in for three counts and out for three counts. As your belly rises and falls, continue to guide your boat. After a few cycles of slow and steady breathing, imagine your boat has safely landed on the shore.

Now bring your attention back to the rise and fall of your belly as you breathe in and out, in and out. Begin to notice how you feel. Is your breathing different than it was when you first started? Does your body feel different? What about your mind? Is it sleepy or full of thoughts? Is it calm? Again, there is no right or wrong answer. When you feel ready, slowly open your eyes. If you were lying down, gently bring yourself to a seated position. Say something kind to yourself:

You are wonderful.

You are special.

You are peace.

You have just practiced mindfulness.

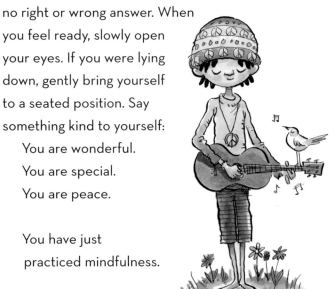